ARIZONA

P9-DNW-829

Text by
JERRY CAMARILLO DUNN, JR.

Photographs by
ANDREA PISTOLESI

BONECHI

© by CASA EDITRICE BONECHI, Via Cairoli, 18/b Florence - Italy
Tel. 055/576841 - Fax 055/5000766
E-mail: bonechi@bonechi.it - Internet: www.bonechi.it

New York Address:
98 Thompson Street # 38 - New York, N.Y. 10012
Ph: (212) 343-9235 - Fax: (212) 625-9636 - e-mail: bonechinyc@aol.com

Project and editorial conception: Casa Editrice Bonechi
Publication Manager: Monica Bonechi
Picture research: Monica Bonechi
Graphic design and make-up: Laura Settesoldi
Cover: Sonia Gottardo. *Editing:* Anna Baldini. *Map:* Riccardo Fattori

Text by
Jerry Camarillo Dunn, Jr.

Team work. All rights reserved. No part of this publication may be reproduced or transmitted in any form or by any means, electronic, chemical or mechanical, including photocopying, recording, or by any information storage and retrieval system, without permission in writing from the publisher. The cover, layout and artwork by the Casa Editrice Bonechi graphic artists in this publication are protected by international copyright.

Photographs from the archives of Casa Editrice Bonechi taken by
Andrea Pistolesi

ISBN 88-8029-369-9

* * *

CONTENTS

INTRODUCTION

Perhaps more than any other state, Arizona is a land of myth.

Myth: *The state is basically a desert, a huge blast furnace, a desolate waste of sand.*

Fact: *Arizona boasts a wonderfully varied landscape and climate. True, in the southern part of the state you'll find broad deserts that are blazing hot in summer. But, all around the state, mountain ranges soar skyward, crowned by 12,633-foot-tall Humphrey's Peak. In the north and east, vast forests grow. Arizona's spectacular red-rock country includes one of the world's natural wonders, the magnificent Grand Canyon — which was carved by a river.*

The myth that Arizona is "all desert" probably arose because the first outsiders traveled across the southern swath, a place of cactus and sand, scorching heat, and sometimes death. From their early reports, people got a clear but mistaken idea of Arizona, reinforced later by some of the state's place names. More than 50 chunks of Arizona geography include the blistering word "hell," from Hellgate Mountain to Hell Hole Valley — a tally that no other state can match. But remember that in Arizona you'll also find Paradise Valley. Not to mention mountain streams and lakes, cool canyons, and many other surprises.

Myth: *Few animals and plants can survive in this "endless desert." Only the poisonous rattlesnake slithers over the dunes. Only the thorny saguaro cactus is silhouetted against the sunset sky.*

Fact: *While it is true that 11 types of rattlesnakes live here, to say nothing of stinging scorpions, venomous black-widow spiders, and poisonous lizards called Gila monsters, Arizona also has gentler creatures. The state's varied elevations create homes for birds and animals that range from roadrunners to Steller's jays, from jackrabbits to elk. Plants include not only prickly pear cactuses in the Lower Sonoran Zone, but also blue spruces and alpine plants in the highest mountains.*

Let's look at Arizona — the real Arizona — a bit more closely.

REGIONS OF ARIZONA

*Reduced to its essentials, Arizona divides into two main provinces: the elevated Colorado Plateau in the north and northeast, occupying nearly half the state, and the Basin and Range country occupying the remainder. The **Colorado Plateau** rises from 4,500 to 10,000 feet and is cut by numerous canyons. The famous Grand Canyon was carved by the Colorado River, which crosses the plateau on its 700-mile journey through the state. Above the plateau rise volcanic cinder cones (such as Sunset Crater) and the lofty San Francisco Peaks, the state's tallest mountain range.*

You'll also find deserts in the Colorado Plateau Province. To the northeast lies the Great Basin Desert, vast and powerful. Canyons cleave the landscape. Black Mesa rises. Haunting Monument Valley offers a timeless display of red-rock spires and buttes (a familiar landscape seen in western movies). At the province's northwestern edge, the parched Mojave Desert is identified by its shrubby creosote bushes and by Joshua trees that grow 30 feet high. As a dividing line at the southern edge of the Colorado Plateau, the Mogollon Rim forms a wall of cliffs that plummet some 2,000 feet straight down.

*The **Basin and Range Province**, as the name implies, is a succession of depressions and mountain ranges. These were created by fracturing and tilting of the earth's rocky crust. In Arizona, mountains higher than about 9,000 feet are often termed "sky islands" or "biological islands"; their cool climate creates a home for Douglas fir forests where squirrels chatter and black bears roam. On Mount Lemmon, in the Santa Catalina Mountains, you can take a remarkable* journey up one of these sky islands. Having begun your drive in the Lower Sonoran Zone among saguaro and cholla cactuses, you climb through junipers and pinyons, enter pine forests, and finally reach the heights where white firs and quaking aspens grow. This journey of only 40 miles is said to be like driving from Mexico to Canada in an hour.

To the Native Americans of Arizona, mountains are often sacred places, the homes of spirits. One such holy place is Baboquivari Peak, southwest of Tucson. Among Anglos the ragged Superstition Mountains gave rise to another sort of mystery: the legend of the Lost Dutchman Mine. It's said that a fabulous gold strike was made here by two German prospectors, one of whom left puzzling directions to their mine before he died in 1891. In the hundred years since then, countless gold hunters have combed the Superstitions in search of the lost mine.

The portion of the province that lies in southern Arizona consists of two distinct deserts. An edge of the Chihuahuan Desert, to the southeast, rises to about 1,500 feet, an altitude where the air cools a little and grass can grow on the hills. In this region are two outlandish sights: a mountain range that is simply an immense pile of boulders (Texas Canyon), and a former lake bed called the Willcox Playa that stretches for 50 square miles, as flat as a griddle, where you literally can't see a thing growing. This place does fit the popular myth of Arizona as an "arid zone," where nothing lives.

In contrast, the Sonoran Desert receives more rain than any other desert on the North American continent. Forests of mesquite grow, and about 300 different bird species thrive. Because it is so scenic, the Sonoran Desert has also attracted 3.1 million human residents, while the state's other regions combined have only half a million people.

PREHISTORIC INDIANS

Some 12,000 to 15,000 years ago, the first residents of Arizona arrived. Bands of hunters armed with stone-tipped spears, these Paleo-Indians came in pursuit of large animals, such as bison and mammoths, and wild plant foods. Without art or building skills, however, they left almost no trace of themselves.

As the climate grew warmer and drier, sometime around 9000 B.C. most of the big animals vanished. A new culture appeared, hunting smaller animals and gathering nuts, seeds, and berries. They made a great technological jump forward between 2000 and 500 B.C. — agriculture. The Indians planted and harvested corn, squash, and beans, providing themselves a diet of high protein and balanced nutrition.

Beginning in perhaps 200 B.C., groups of these ancient people began to build villages. They lived in "pithouses," each a shallow pit beneath a wooden frame that was filled in with mud plaster to make walls. By trading, these people gathered not only goods but also ideas from outside their home territories. Religion appeared, directed toward rainfall and the harvest. Art flourished. The most prominent of these early farming cultures were the Hohokam (southern deserts), the Mogollon (mountain valleys in the eastern uplands), the Anasazi (high deserts on the Colorado Plateau), and the Sinagua (Verde Valley, southern Colorado Plateau).

Between A.D. 500 and 1100 Arizona's early cultures made further leaps forward. In architecture, they built homes above the ground in pueblo style. In trade, they collected everything from parrot feathers to copper bells. In culture, they learned to grow and weave cotton, created complex towns, conducted elaborate spiritual ceremonies, made pottery decorated with sophisticated images of birds and lizards, and even dug irrigation ditches in the Salt and Gila River valleys. By A.D. 1350 the Hohokam were erecting high-rise buildings, and today you can visit the ruins of four-story Casa Grande (Big House), which scientists figure may have been an observatory for marking the solstices, and possibly a residence for a top level of Hohokam society, perhaps priests or elite leaders.

At the same time, the Anasazi ("Ancient Ones") made great advances in northeastern Arizona. Their cities, built in the protective alcoves of towering sandstone cliffs, fit into their stone settings like jewels into a crown. These pueblos consisted of apartments, large and communal. Most had ceremonial rooms called kivas, where religious rituals and social gatherings took place. Despite their success, however, the Anasazi vanished around A.D. 1300, followed by the Hohokam and other major cultures of early Arizona. No one has been able to fathom why this happened, although drought may have led them to abandon their villages. Today, powerful aura seems to exist around the old homes of the Anasazi, something almost ghostly. Perhaps this explains why the Najavo never moved into the abandoned Anasazi cities.

Arizona is one of the few places where you can have a direct experence of America's most distant past. Its ruins surround you. Spectacular Anasazi ruins stand in Canyon de Chelly National Monument. The Sinagua (who may have blended Anasazi and Hohokam cultures) left ruins at Casa Grande, Montezuma Castle, Wupatki, Walnut Canyon, and Tuzigoot National Monuments.

THE SPANISH ARRIVE

A myth lured the early Spaniards to Arizona. The Seven Cities of Cibola were said to be built of gold. When the explorer Francisco Vásquez de Coronado arrived in Arizona around 1540, however, he found only houses built of sun-baked mud, not shining gold, and they were occupied by hostile Indians. This shattered the fable of the "golden cities," and a century passed without further interest from the Spanish government. Spanish religion arrived, however, as Franciscan padres established missions among the Hopi. In the early 1700s the Jesuit Padre Eusebio Kino founded missions in southern Arizona among the Pimas and Papagos. When mistreatment led the peaceful Pimas to revolt in 1751, the Spanish built a military garrison (or presidio), at Tubac to control the area.

The Spanish period ended in 1821, when Mexico declared its independence from Spain. Anglo fur trappers and traders began to pass through, and two decades later these "mountain men" guided parties of U.S. Army explorers and surveyors. The ownership of Arizona was decided in the Mexican War of 1848, when most of Arizona was ceded to the United States. With the Gadsden Purchase of 1853, the state's southern section was also added.

During the California Gold Rush, many Forty-Niners had crossed the southern stretch of Arizona via the Gila Trail, but few settled down — that is, until a gold strike occurred in 1857 on the Gila River. Fortune seekers flooded in, and to feed them, settlers came to raise crops and cattle. By 1863 a U.S. territory called Arizona was declared. (The name may derive from a 1736 silver strike in a gulch the Indians called Arizonac.) The new government's most pressing business was to subjugate the hostile Apaches and Navajos. Indian wars raged from 1871 to 1886, when the Chiracahua Apache leader, Geronimo, finally surrendered. The U.S. government removed him and his people to a Florida prison camp.

During this time, cattle ranchers grazed their herds, Mormons established farms, and miners at Tombstone dug up silver ore worth $19 million in ten years. Copper was also discovered, with the proceeds helping to build Victorian towns like Jerome, Globe, and Bisbee. In the 1870s and 1880s railroads arrived in Arizona. The modern era was dawning.

TODAY'S ARIZONA

After Arizona attained statehood in 1912, as the 48th state, copper mining provided a solid economic base, while dams in the middle of the state made farming and city growth possible. During World War II, Army air bases and defense industries came to Arizona, and after the armistice many soldiers and workers returned to the state to live. Between 1950 and 1970 the population more than doubled. Because of Arizona's warm winter weather (and the advent of air-conditioning for summer comfort), retirees also flocked to the state.

Today Arizona is a remarkable conglomeration — part boomtown economy (especially in tourism and manufacturing), part living museum of the American West (with real cowboys and more Indians than any other state), and part scenic wonderland, from the floor of the Grand Canyon to the summit of the highest peak.

TUCSON

Even though Tucson is Arizona's second-largest city, with 675,000 people, it has retained a small-town feeling and a distinctly human scale. Many visitors choose to park their cars and see the city on foot. Tucson's relaxed mood suits a place that is both a resort and a college town. This mood may derive from the city's climate — which is milder than Phoenix's, due to its elevation of 2,400 feet — and its natural surroundings. Tucson lies in a desert valley, ringed by four ranges of mountains. To the north, the Santa Catalinas rear up, all ragged granite and gneiss; to the east, the Rincons are smoothly rounded; to the south, the Santa Ritas rise with twin peaks; to the west stand the small, sawtoothed Tucsons. The city has an intimate connection with its encircling mountains. In an hour, residents can drive from Tucson's desert valley of paloverde and mesquite trees to the slopes of Mount Lemmon, where summer hikers find wildflower meadows and winter fun-seekers enjoy the nation's southernmost ski area.

Spaniards first heard the name Tucson when they met Pima Indians dwelling in a village called *Stukshon*, meaning "at the foot of dark mountain." (The dark mountain is now known as Sentinel Peak.) When Spanish soldiers returned in 1776 to build a garrison, they adapted the village's name for their fortress, the Presidio San Augustín del Tucson. The fort had adobe walls 12 feet high and 3 feet thick for protection from marauding Apaches.

Despite the danger of Indian raids and the harshness of the desert, Anglo-Americans came to settle. By the 1850s the Butterfield stage line had reached Tucson, ushering in a colorful Wild West era complete with outlaws and gunfights in the streets. The growing city was officially incorporated in 1864. But when the territorial legislature later handed out major construction projects, Phoenix got the supposed prizes — an insane asylum and a prison — while Tucson was allotted a university. The rough, unpolished citizens of Tucson sneered at this notion of an institution, and the official who announced it at a public meeting found himself dodging a barrage of eggs, spoiled vegetables, and even a deceased cat.

Protected by mountains, Tucson is a haven for sun-seekers, college students, and people who enjoy Indian and Spanish history.

Historic buildings in the El Presidio neighborhood vary from grand Spanish Colonial architecture (above) to simple houses (right).

But a saloon keeper and two gamblers soon donated land for the university campus. (Legend says that their "donation" was prompted by a losing hand in a card game.) In 1891 the **University of Arizona** opened with just 32 students and 6 faculty members, who met in a brick building called Old Main (which you can visit today). Other attractions around the 325-acre campus include the university art museum (Jacques Lipchitz sculptures), the Arizona State Museum (prehistoric and modern Indian artifacts), the Center for Creative Photography (20th-century masters, particularly Ansel Adams), and a planetarium (16-inch telescope for observing the clear desert skies).

To see the face of Tucson past, visit the **Barrio Histórico**, a district of 13 square blocks with 150 adobe buildings from the late 1800s. Nearby, have a

The old Pima County Courthouse echoes Spanish and Moorish designs, with a splash of the American Southwest.

look at the sandstone façade of the **St. Augustine Cathedral** of 1896, inspired by Mexico's Cathedral of Querétero.

Also stroll around **El Presidio**, a downtown neighborhood whose many historical buildings and residences clearly show the city's Spanish, Mexican, and American influences. The adobe **John C. Frémont House Museum** is where the territorial governor may (or may not) have lived in 1881; its furnishings evoke the life of an upper-class family of the period. **El Presidio Park** occupies the drill field of the long-gone Spanish fortress. Part of the old presidio wall is on view at the adjacent **Pima County Courthouse**, whose tile dome and striking architecture combine Spanish, Moorish, and Southwest designs.

Spanish Colonial paintings and furnishings are exhibited at the **Tucson Museum of Art**, along with pre-Columbian pieces. The **Arizona Historical Society Museum** displays 3,000 artifacts, from the prehistoric Hohokam through the Spanish, mountain men, cattle ranchers, and other figures who followed; a mock-up of a copper mine has a tunnel, equipment, and even sound effects. Moving into the modern era, the **Pima Air Museum** shows off some 150 aircraft, among them an X-15, the world's fastest jet airplane. At the **Titan Missile Museum** you'll see a nuclear command post and the world's only disarmed intercontinental ballistic missile that is displayed in its underground silo.

Other **things to see and do** in Tucson include a modest zoo, a botanical garden, the 17,000-acre Tucson Mountain Park, and tours of Davis-Monthan Air Force Base (where bomber crews trained in World War II). Visitors who enjoy cultural activities can attend the ballet, symphony, or events at the university. Shoppers can explore the galleries and stores downtown, see Native American crafts and Mexican imports, or buy a pair of genuine cowboy boots and a big Stetson hat. Ted DeGrazia's Gallery in the Sun, a museum located in the home of the late, well-known Arizona artist, displays his sentimental

St. Augustine Cathedral, with its delicate sandstone façade, dates to 1896. Above the door, a bronze statue of the saint welcomes visitors.

The "Gallery in the Sun" museum of the late painter Ted DeGrazia is open to visitors.

paintings of Southwest Indian and Hispanic life. One highly publicized attraction is **Biosphere 2**, an immense glass building that contains a self-enclosed world with its own desert, marsh, ocean, rainforest, and farms. Biosphere 2, designed to recycle or produce its own air, food, and water, with nearly 4,000 species of plants and animals, is used as a research center run by Columbia University. Scientists hope the project will yield information useful for saving earth's environment and for human survival during extended space travel. Visitors are welcome to observe and learn about current experiments.

However, most travelers probably would rather enjoy the outdoor environment of Tucson, a natural world with endless miles of blue skies, desert beauty, and lofty mountains. Tucson lacks rivers, but is criss-crossed by a system of arroyos, or gulches, that rush with water during rains. These arroyos nurture enough living things that scientists have termed them "xeroriparian" habitats, a ten-dollar word that means "dry riverbank" zone. The arroyos support mesquite and paloverde trees and so bring desert scenery right into the city.

Tucson's natural beauty and its yearly 320 days of sunshine explain why **golf** is such a popular sport here. A number of resorts boast fine courses, among them the picturesque Sheraton El Conquistador, the highly rated Westin La Paloma, and the well-designed Loews Ventana Canyon course. There are also a number of public courses, as well as many tennis courts. Tucson is also a hub for **dude ranches** — don't forget, this is the American Southwest — where you can go horseback riding on rustic trails. You can also try hiking, rock-hounding, bird-watching, and bicycling on paths throughout the urban area.

And after you've seen the sights of the city, your journey is just beginning, for Tucson is the gateway to the rest of southern Arizona.

Colorful flowers and lush turf flourish on the desert at the Sheraton El Conquistador (below and opposite), one of many golf resorts around Tucson.

OLD TUCSON STUDIOS

The dusty streets and frontier buildings of Old Tucson should look mighty familiar to movie fans. About 250 westerns have been made here, including the classics *Gunfight at the OK Corral* and *Rio Lobo*. It's no wonder that Old Tucson calls itself "Hollywood in the Desert." As a sort of combination movie set and theme park, Old Tucson isn't a historically accurate rendering of a Wild West town. But it has been an important part of movie history. When Columbia Pictures was preparing to shoot *Arizona* in 1939, the producers spent a quarter of a million dollars to create Old Tucson. Nowadays, you'll see what appears to be a dusty Arizona town of the 1860s, with saloons, wooden sidewalks, false-front buildings, a frontier mission, and a Mexican plaza. Old Tucson has been a backdrop for westerns that range from *The Last Outpost* (starring Ronald Reagan) to such television series as "High Chaparral" and "Little House on the Prairie." During your visit, you may see a movie, TV show, or commercial being filmed.

Old Tucson is located 12 miles west of the city in Tucson Mountain Park. It opened as a public attraction in 1958. To entertain visitors, "outlaws" still stage shootouts in the street (using blank cartridges, of course). You can tour a movie soundstage, ride a rattling ore wagon through an "old mine," visit a museum of historic firearms, and admire an 1872 steam locomotive used by the Virginia & Truckee Railroad. There's also a musical review and even an 1870s-style magic show.

Old Tucson Studios (also on following pages) has been the location of numerous western movies. It has been restored after a recent fire.

ARIZONA-SONORA DESERT MUSEUM

Rattlesnakes, prairie dogs, bighorn sheep, cactus wrens - more than 200 species of Sonoran Desert animals and birds are displayed in their natural surroundings at this living museum. Ranked among the world's top ten zoos, it offers an easy-to-grasp portrait of a desert environment that stretches from Arizona southward into Mexico and around the Gulf of California. Surprisingly, the Sonoran Desert of Arizona includes mountains and rivers, so you'll see mountain lions, playful otters, and industrious beavers at the museum, too. In size, the creatures here range from a tiny calliope hummingbird (weighing one tenth of an ounce) to a lumbering black bear.

You can go below ground to view desert animals in their burrows. The Earth Sciences Center displays mineral specimens and meteorites, while the museum gardens embrace a broad spectrum of Sonoran Desert plants, including springtime wildflowers. From the museum there is a fine view of the surrounding desert and Baboquivari and Kitt Peaks.

Visitors are amazed at the wildlife concealed in the desert but on view at this fine museum.

SAN XAVIER DEL BAC

One glance at the sublime beauty of this Spanish Baroque mission reveals why it is affectionately called the "White Dove of the Desert." It rises on the desert floor like a bird taking flight. The tireless Padre Eusebio Francisco Kino established the mission in 1700, later observing: "Anybody might have [founded it], but His whisper came to me." The name derives from San Xavier, who was Kino's patron, and from Bac, a Tohono O'odham (Papago) village whose name means "where the water emerges."

After the original mission was destroyed, the present church of 1797 was built of fired adobe bricks and plastered with white stucco. No one knows why the right-hand tower was never finished, however. The two best theories: 1) Symbolically, its incompleteness proclaims that the preaching of the Gospel is never concluded; 2) The builders ran short of funds.

San Xavier del Bac stands among the Southwest's most perfect examples of Spanish Colonial architecture. Between the two towers rises an astoundingly ornate stone portal.

Look closely and you'll find arches and scrolls, saints and seashells, even a cat and a rat. The interior is highly decorative for a mission church, with a frescoed dome, statues, and a stunningly carved polychrome retablo. Such beauty also had a practical purpose: The captain of Tucson's Spanish presidio noted that the Jesuits intended their church "to attract by its loveliness the unconverted [Indians] beyond the frontier."

Since Arizona was indeed a frontier, building materials were scarce. Lacking marble, the builders painted the altar in imitation of it; lacking glazed tiles, they painted the dados to resemble them. Even "chandeliers" were painted on the walls to supplement the few real ones available for the church. Architects and critics have sought superlatives to describe San Xavier del Bac. One called it the "Sistine Chapel of the United States." Another pronounced the mission "the most beautiful man-made object in America Deserta."

In recent years the mission has been meticulously and beautifully restored by artisans using original building techniques and materials.

Called the "White Dove of the Desert," Mission San Xavier del Bac was a religious outpost in the Arizona wilderness (also on following pages).

SAGUARO NATIONAL PARK

The saguaro cactus is the symbol of Arizona, and its blossom is the state flower. But that's not why people love the saguaro. This cactus looks familiar — like a tall, skinny person — and strangely friendly. Its waving arms seem to say, "Howdy, pardner." To protect the much-loved saguaro (sah-WAH-roh), a plant found only in the Sonoran Desert, this park was established in two sections on either side of the city of Tucson.

To the west the 21,000-acre **Tucson Mountains Unit** has vast stands of saguaros. Stop at the new **visitors center**, whose exhibits help you understand the plants and animals that live just outside the window. You'll learn that nature designed the saguaro to store water; it resembles a barrel whose pleats can expand like an accordion. In spring it flowers with cream-colored blossoms, and in midsummer the fruit appears. The visitors center is also a good place to ask directions to Signal Hill, where the prehistoric Hohokam left intriguing petroglyphs.

The park's 62,000-acre eastern section, the **Rincon Mountain Unit**, displays saguaro cactuses against the scenic backdrop of Rincon Peak and Mica Mountain. Until 1958, young cactuses in this area were being crushed by grazing cattle, which have since been cleared out. Today you'll find only very young and old saguaros here. The cactus grows slowly, and after 25 years may stand only 2 feet tall. At maturity, however, it can tower 50 feet high and weigh 10 tons. By old age, at around 150 years, the cactus may have as many as 40 arms. A saguaro can live for 200 years.

You pass through five different climate zones in Saguaro National Park East. To see the area, take the **Cactus Forest Drive** in the foothills of the Rincon Mountains; it leads to several picnic areas, a desert ecology trail, a nature trail, and wilderness hiking

Rising to heights of 50 feet, the saguaro cactus is protected in this reserve (also on following pages).

trails. Everywhere you will see saguaros, desert monarchs that rule quietly over a silent kingdom. A wordless mystery also abides in the park. At **Signal Hill** you can walk a short interpretive trail to a hilltop where the Hohokam left petroglyphs, or images pecked into the rocks.

The designs appear on rocks layered with desert varnish, a natural dark patina of manganese and iron oxide that was easy to scratch through and provided a contrasting background. There are images of human hands, arrows, concentric circles, and what appear to be suns.

The petroglyphs may have served as written notice that certain clans were in the area, or may have indicated water sources. As no one alive today can read their meaning, they remain enigmas.

The petroglyphs on Signal Hill also can't be dated accurately. (There are others throughout the national park.) The Hohokam culture was centered in the Salt River Valley near Phoenix, where these ancient Indians had a rather sophisticated civilization based on irrigated agriculture. But their territory extended south to the area around present-day Tucson. Why they left their marks here, no one knows.

Signal Hill in Saguaro National Park preserves the mysterious designs of the Hohokam.

KITT PEAK OBSERVATORY

They appear atop Kitt Peak like strange white flowers — and it is not by accident that these astronomical observatories grow here. Before choosing this 6,900-foot-high peak, scientists made a study of 150 mountaintops around the Southwest. They were looking for a place where skies that were free of pollution from dust and city lights would create ideal conditions for star-gazing. Here the sky is remarkably clear.

Kitt Peak rises on the 2.75-million-acre Tohono O'odham (Papago) Indian reservation, whose leaders agreed to accept this national observatory on their tribal lands back in the late 1950s. More than 20 universities now cooperatively manage the facility, which is funded by the National Science Foundation. The white domes shelter advanced instruments that probe the mysteries of the cosmos. Stop first at the museum to see exhibits on astronomy, light, and the technology of modern star-gazing. Then take a tour of some of Kitt Peak's 21 telescopes. The world's largest solar telescope is the McMath. You can't directly view the sun through it, of course. But visitors can examine the instrument itself, which employs mirrors arrayed in a 500-foot-long corridor (partly above ground and mostly below) to create an image of the sun that measures 30 inches across. The McMath's design won an architectural award.

Other instruments on Kitt Peak are designed not to magnify images but to gather light from distant, faint sources. The 2.1-meter telescope takes in both visible light and infrared radiation to yield information about faraway stars and galaxies. The Mayall 4-meter telescope occupies a building 19 stories high, and you must take an elevator to see it. (The 10th-floor observation deck has a view over southern Arizona, a desert world of cactus and mesquite, ironwood and paloverde trees.) Other instruments used here employ radio waves for observing the heavens. As a group, Kitt Peak's telescopes make up one of the world's most important astronomical centers.

Atop Kitt Peak stands one of the world's great collections of instruments for observing the universe beyond our earth.

TUMACACORI MISSION

Once a spiritual hub for the Pima Indians, San José de Tumacacori mission is now a weathered ruin of adobe walls. But it is easy to discern the mission's former grandeur, which results from its architectural style — Spanish Colonial Baroque — and building materials. There are graceful arches, portals, and cornices. A three-story bell tower rises above the baptistry, whose adobe walls are nine feet thick.

In a sense, the mission dates back to 1691, when Padre Kino founded a mission outpost (called a *visita*) in the nearby Pima village, Tumacacori. The Jesuits were later succeeded by the Franciscans, and Padre Gutiérrez resolved to erect a church to rival the celebrated San Xavier del Bac, starting work around 1800. The church opened to worshipers by 1822, although it was never really finished. The independent Mexican government cut off funding for missionary work, and in 1848 the mission closed because Apache raids plagued it continually. The friars and parishioners brought the church's furnishings to San Xavier del Bac.

Before being declared a national monument in 1908, the mission fell to ruins, a fate hastened by treasure hunters. Believing tales that the priests had left great riches, they ransacked the mission — and found nothing.

Today San José de Tumacacori is preserved as a historic park. A museum displays original wooden statues from the church. You can also see the storeroom, mortuary chapel, cemetery, and other areas. The patio garden is a quiet haven filled with fruit trees, herbs, and flowers, all typical of the region's 18th-century Spanish missions.

Ask the park staff about church services and festivals held at Tumacacori in the Christmas season, spring, and fall.

They can also advise when visitors are able to see the ruins of two other Spanish missions now being excavated nearby — Calabazas and Guévavi. With just a bit of imagination, you can look at all these adobe ruins and see a living picture of mission life in days gone by.

Now a picturesque ruin of adobe, San José de Tumacacori mission is preserved as a historical park.

TOMBSTONE

The town of Tombstone is like a history book of the Wild West — with bullet holes shot through the covers. Gambling dens, saloons, dance halls, brothels; this town had them all. Not to mention the most notorious gunfight in western history.

It all started in 1877 in Apache territory, where a wandering prospector named Ed Schieffelin left Fort Huachuca looking for silver and gold. His scornful friends said that in this dangerous territory he would find ''nothing but his tombstone.'' Yet he struck silver, choosing (with a touch of irony) to name his claim ''Tombstone.'' When he later discovered one of Arizona's richest silver lodes, his brother commented, ''You're a lucky cuss.'' With customary flair, Shieffelin named his find the Lucky Cuss Mine. (He also named the Good Enough and Tough Nut Mines.) By the time the silver gave out in this district after the turn of the century, miners had extracted $40 million in ore.

Such wealth lured prospectors, outlaws, upright citizens, drunks, whores, hard-working miners, and adventurers of all kinds. A settlement grew up, incorporated in 1879, and soon had 5,000 citizens. With its newly found riches, Tombstone offered a high degree of luxury, its restaurants serving what was reputed to be the best food between New Orleans and San Francisco. (An 1887 menu at the Maison Doree restaurant featured papillote and saddle of lamb à la Milanese.) The town issued more than a hundred liquor licenses.

Citizens flocked to the watering holes, casinos, and whorehouses along **Allen Street**. The town's main avenue, it has been carefully restored. (Japanese film-makers have even shot Samurai westerns here.) As the hub of nightlife, Allen Street was crowned by the **Crystal Palace Saloon**, a luxurious barroom and gambling hall built in 1879. You'll see its original pressed-tin ceiling (a common feature of western commercial buildings) and a replica of the mahogany bar. Sometimes five bartenders at once were needed to serve the throng of drinkers. You can still get a shot of whiskey here, and the bar is even equipped with old-fashioned moustache towels.

Also visit the **Bird Cage Theater**, whose doors never closed during the first three years after it opened in 1881. The adobe building housed a stage show, casino, saloon, and brothel. It was named for stalls shaped like birdcages, which hung from the ceiling and showed off the resident "ladies of the evening." At the legendary Bird Cage, history's longest-running poker game was played, lasting 8 years, 5 months, and 3 days. You can see the poker room and its original furniture. You can also amuse yourself by examining some of the 140 bullet holes that perforate the ceiling and walls of this establishment.

The wild life and boomtown growth of Tombstone were documented by the local newspaper, which began publication in 1880 at the **Tombstone** *Epitaph* **Office**. (John Clum, the paper's editor and founder, commented that "no tombstone is complete without its epitaph.") Visit the office to see the newspaper's original presses

Gunfighters, gamblers, stagecoach rides — all part of the fun at historic Tombstone.

and early issues of the paper. Editorially, the *Epitaph* took the side of the Earp brothers after their famous shootout with the Clantons at the **OK Corral**, a site that is the main attraction in Tombstone. The most famous gunfight in Wild West history took place here in October 1881. Historians can't agree on the precise details, but the fight resulted from a long-running feud in Cochise County. One camp consisted of Sheriff Johnny Behan and Ike Clanton's gang of "ranchers," who engaged in

extracurricular cattle rustling. This activity undermined the power of U.S. deputy marshals Virgil, Wyatt, and Morgan Earp, who formed the other camp with their friend, the tubercular, alcoholic, gunfighting dentist John "Doc" Holliday. In the early afternoon of October 26, the two sides met at the OK Corral. Wyatt Earp said, "You sons-of-bitches, you have been looking for a fight, and now you can have it." The two sides opened fire with shotguns and pistols at close range for 30 seconds. At the end,

Notorious Boothill Cemetery is the final resting place of badmen who died at the OK Corral.

three of the Clanton gang lay dying, and both Virgil and Morgan Earp were wounded. The Earps faced charges in court, but were freed by a judge who found the killings "fully justified" as part of the lawmen's duties. Today, a tourist can "walk where they fell" and see life-size mannequins placed where the gunfighters stood.

Your logical next stop would be the **Boothill Cemetery**, since that's where the three Clantons were buried after being "hurled into eternity," as the *Epitaph* phrased it. The hilltop cemetery, which overlooks Tombstone and the desert, is the final resting place of at least 250 people, many of whom were murdered, hanged, killed by Indians, or on the losing end of gunfights. Among the occupants are a popular prostitute named Dutch Annie, and John Heath, an accused murderer whom a mob lynched in 1884. (The coroner reported that he perished of "strangulation, self-inflicted or otherwise.") You can wander around the cemetery, reading colorful tombstones that capture the essence of life and

death in the Old West: "Here Lies Lester Moore/Four Slugs/From a 44/No Les/No More." Another is "George Johnson — Hanged by Mistake."

Frontier justice — such as it was — was meted out at the **Tombstone Courthouse**. Because Tombstone ranked as the biggest town between St. Louis and San Francisco, it became the seat of Cochise County, a status that required erecting an official courthouse. Built of red brick in 1882, the two-story, Victorian Neoclassical structure is now a state historic park. It houses a reconstruction of the courtroom, with the original judge's bench and prisoner's dock.

A more benign sort of landmark is the **Rose Tree Inn**, a former miners' boardinghouse and hotel that takes its name from a Lady Banksia rosebush planted in 1885. Since then it has spread over some 8,000 square feet, claiming a mention in the *Guinness Book of World Records* as the world's largest rosebush. Look for its white blossoms in

The most famous gunfight in the West took place in 1881 at the notorious corral in Tombstone.

At Tombstone Courthouse (1882), the judge's gavel once hammered out frontier justice.

spring. The inn now functions as a museum, with rooms displaying period furnishings that belonged to an 1880s pioneer.

Other attractions in Tombstone include Arizona's oldest existing Protestant church, St. Paul's Episcopal, built in 1881. Shieffelin Hall is an 1881 adobe building where touring theater companies staged plays and boxing champion John L. Sullivan performed exhibition bouts. The early days of Tombstone are presented in dioramas at the Arizona Territorial Museum, while Historama uses film and animated figures to tell the town's story. The Fly Exhibition Gallery shows the work of early photographer C.S. Fly, including a portrait of the Apache leader Geronimo. You can also tour the Good Enough Mine.

Among the town's hardest-to-miss attractions are the gunfights and barroom brawls staged by various costumed badmen. As you listen to the pop of pistol fire and see the bodies fall, you may get an idea of what Tombstone was like in the good (?) old days.

BISBEE

When a prospector discovered copper around Mule Pass Gulch in 1875, he was less than thrilled. He had been seeking gold or silver and left without even staking a claim. A couple of years later an Army scout named Jack Dunn also struck copper. He filed a claim, but lost it on a drunken bet that he could outrun a man on horseback. (Needless to say, he couldn't.) Eventually, the Copper Queen mine was developed by Judge DeWitt Bisbee and outside investors. Then the East Coast Phelps Dodge Company bought the adjoining land, and to avoid legal wrangling over ore, the two companies merged.

A substantial town grew from the original mining camp. A miner's shack housed a school, although students occasionally had to hide in a nearby mine tunnel when hostile Indians were spied in the vicinity. Sin was generally confined to **Brewery Gulch**, a side canyon lined with casinos, brothels, and saloons. Since the brewery sluiced its dregs down the gutter, the street was "covered with a slime several inches deep." By 1900 Bisbee had become the biggest and richest city in Arizona, with 20,000 residents. Mining didn't stop till 1975, having yielded $2 billion.

You can put on a hard hat and slicker for a mine-car tour of the underground **Copper Queen Mine**, which has 143 miles of tunnels. Or visit the **Lavender Open Pit Mine**, a huge hole in the ground created by the removal of hundreds of million of tons of dirt and ore. The **Bisbee Mining and Historical Museum** recounts local history and explains copper mining through old equipment and dioramas; the museum occupies the 1897 headquarters of the Copper Queen mining company. The **Bisbee Restoration and Historical Society Museum** also displays pieces of the past, from household furnishings to a blackjack table from a Brewery Gulch saloon.

The still-operating 1902 **Copper Queen Hotel** harks back to the days when Bisbee was an exciting destination for all stripes of people, from mining moguls and politicians to lucky prospectors spending their loot.

Boom and bust in Bisbee depended on the copper mines, which produced till 1975. Today much of the historic town looks as it did in the late 1800s.

CHIRICAHUA NATIONAL MONUMENT

Here is the traditional home of Cochise and the Chiricahua Apaches, who called this region the "Land of the Standing-Up Rocks." Volcanic rock, fractured by the force of slow uplifting over many millennia, has eroded into remarkable formations — towers, balanced rocks, needles. For a good overview, take the **Bonita Canyon Drive**, which climbs six miles over the north end of the Chiricahua Mountains to 6,870-foot Massai Point, where there is a panoramic view over cracked lava beds. From here you can walk the easy **Massai Point Nature Trail** or the 3.5-mile **Echo Canyon Trail** loop. The **Heart of Rocks Trail** takes you to oddly shaped (and named) formations like Duck on a Rock, and Punch and Judy.

The terrain throughout the 12,000-acre national monument is best seen on foot. Other **trails** include the Rhyolite Canyon Nature Trail, devoted to native plant life, and the Faraway Meadow Trail, a good place for bird-watching. To better understand what you're seeing, stop in at the **visitor center**, whose displays focus on the local environment, geology, and wildlife. The surrounding area is the haunt of numerous black bears, as well as deer, peccaries, coatimundis, and lizards. The forest trees of the Chiricahua Mountains include Douglas fir, ponderosa pine, oak, cypress, and aspen. If you visit in the summertime, you'll find this season surprisingly rainy; almost every afternoon brings a thundershower. You can also learn about local history. After the surrender of the Chiricahua Apaches, a family of Swedish settlers moved into Bonita Canyon and worked a homestead they called **Faraway Ranch**. Neil and Emma Erickson, their daughter, Lillian, and her husband operated it as a guest ranch. The family dwelled on the land for 91 years, until the National Park Service bought it in 1979. Today you can tour the ranch house and outbuildings, finding out about pioneer life at Faraway Ranch — so named, said Lillian Erickson, because it was "god-awful far away from everything."

Stone columns and walls define the landscape at Chiricahua National Monument, once home to the Apaches.

ORGAN PIPE CACTUS N.M.

As you roam these 516 square miles — the largest national monument in Arizona — the Sonoran Desert puts on a theatrical performance. At center stage is the organ pipe cactus, which resembles a saguaro with all its arms stemming directly from the base. The monument has a cast of 31 cactus species, and the rare elephant tree also takes a bow. More than 270 types of birds make an appearance, along with bighorn sheep, kit foxes, bobcats, javelina, kangaroo rats, and lizards.

More than 30 species of cactus live here, including organ pipe cactus and elephant trees (also on following pages).

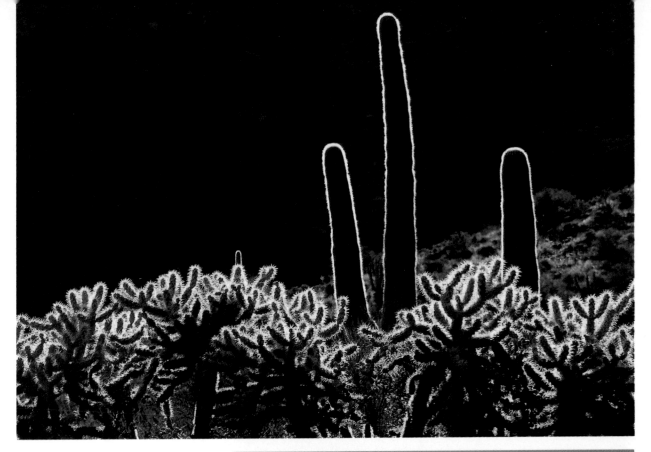

Take the **Puerto Blanco Scenic Drive** to the oasis called Quitobaquito, where a natural spring flows into a pond that is edged with cottonwood trees. Travelers ranging from Padre Kino to Forty-Niners on their way to the California Gold Rush once stopped at this rare water source. They were journeying on what Spaniards called the Camino del Diablo, or "Devil's Highway," across southern Arizona. Today Quitobaquito oasis is visited by migrating ducks and other waterfowl, and coots are year-round residents. Along the drive, Senita Basin is a good place to see elephant trees, which resemble organ pipe cactuses with the addition of gray "whiskers."

The **Ajo Mountain Drive** leads into the rugged foothills of Mount Ajo (4,808 feet), passing stands of organ pipe cactus. (The long arms of these desert plants may

remind you of the pipes of a church organ.) Amid spectacular scenery you can hike the Estes Canyon-Bull Pasture Trail through a canyon and along a ridge, ending up at a pasture once used by cattle ranchers for grazing their stock. From the Desert View Nature Trail you'll see a fine panorama, while the Victoria Mine Trail leads to an abandoned mine that once yielded lead, silver, and gold. But the monument's true treasures, you will find, are spring wildflowers, which are helped to grow by a surprising nine inches of annual rainfall — the purple cups of hedgehog cactuses, the splashy yellow blossoms of the palo verde, magenta owl's clover, blue lupines, apricot mallow, and desert marigolds.

YUMA

Yuma is hot. Very hot. It is said to receive more sunshine than any other city in the United States, which accounts for its popularity among winter "snowbirds" fleeing here from the frozen north, and for its success as a citrus ranching area. It also explains why a prisoner sent to the old Yuma Territorial Prison endured an additional punishment; in summer he would roast in his cell at temperatures up to 120 degrees Fahrenheit. The heat accounts for comments by an 1860s journalist, who reported: "Everything dries; wagons dry; men dry; chickens dry; there is no juice left in any thing, living or dead, by the end of summer... Chickens hatched at this season, old Fort Yumers say, come out of the shell ready cooked...."

Yuma came into existence because of its location on the Colorado River, which (before being dammed) was a true force of nature, some 600 feet wide at its narrowest point. At Yuma the river was shallow enough to allow a safe crossing, as Spanish

Built of stone and adobe, the 1876 Yuma Territorial Prison housed the outlaws of the Wild West, who were jammed in, six to a cell.

The terrain near Yuma — sand dunes bare of plant life — reflects the very hot climate.

explorers discovered in the 1700s. Soldiers and padres built a fort and missions on the far side of the river, but in 1781 the Quechan Indians revolted, killing most of the Spanish colony and ending Spanish control of the Yuma Crossing.

After the U.S. claimed the area in 1846, Colonel Philip Cooke blazed a road through to California, later used by Forty-Niners heading to the gold fields. Indian attacks remained a problem, so in 1851 Fort Yuma was established on the California side of the river. The Yuma Indians were subdued, river steamers began to serve the fort, and a town grew up on the Arizona side. Its name, Yuma, supposedly derives from billows of smoke (called *umo* in old Spanish) rising from fires that local Indians built for rain-making ceremonies.

Arizona Territory was so lawless that decent citizens finally demanded that robbers and murderers be put behind bars. In 1876 the stone-and-adobe **Yuma Territorial Prison** was built, largely by the prisoners themselves. Six of them were packed into each cell,

but despite the discomfort, the prison was considered an enlightened facility, housing Yuma's only library and serving fairly good food. Today you can tour the cellblocks, guard tower, and a museum of photos and artifacts used (and often made) by prisoners.

The story of Yuma's more law-abiding citizens is on display at the Arizona Historical Society, whose **Century House Museum** occupies an 1871 adobe house; the gardens showcase exotic plants and aviary birds. The adjacent Adobe Annex belonged to an 1890s steamboat captain. At the old steamboat landing, visit the **Yuma Quartermaster Depot**, used by the Army until 1883 for resupplying forts in Arizona during the Indian Wars. You can tour the officers' quarters and other buildings. These are restored to the way they looked in 1876, before the arrival of the railroad and the building of Laguna Dam together sank the river steamboat business. The dam did, however, collect the water that made Yuma an important agricultural center.

PHOENIX

When you're in Phoenix, mountains surround you and create what locals call the Valley of the Sun. To the east rise the Superstition Mountains, which may still hide the legendary Lost Dutchman Mine. The South Mountains make up the biggest city park in the world, with 15,000 acres that are ideal for a picnic. Picturesquely named (and shaped) Camelback Mountain rises to the northeast, and Squaw Peak stands right in the city.

At one time this thousand-square-mile valley was home to the Hohokam. As early as 300 B.C., these prehistoric Indians had dug irrigation canals to tame the Salt River and water their fields of cotton, corn, beans, and squash. Some four centuries after the Hohokam mysteriously disappeared around A.D. 1450, those canals were in use again; a former Confederate army officer decided to form a company, dig out the canals, and develop the valley's potential for farming. Within a year he was harvesting wheat and barley.

A settlement grew, and by 1870 it was named Phoenix by an Englishman who prophesized that a city would rise from the ruins of the Hohokam culture, just as the mythical phoenix bird rose from its own ashes. Indeed, the fast-growing town became territorial capital within 20 years.

Because of its setting at the northern edge of the Sonoran Desert, Phoenix needed one thing to grow from a farm town into what has become the nation's ninth largest city — more water. This need was answered in 1911 by Roosevelt Dam. With water available, the cotton industry boomed. Phoenix's stockyards were second only to those in Chicago. In the 1910s East Coast doctors began prescribing dry desert air for patients suffering from respiratory problems, so Phoenix attracted health seekers. Easterners also visited dude ranches to try living like cowboys and riding the range. Winter residents in the 1930s included East Coast magnates such as chewing-gum maker William Wrigley, Jr. and

Glittering Phoenix grew up in the 1870s and just kept growing into the ninth largest city in the U.S., with many cultural and recreational assets.

Phoenix's cathedral stands against the pure blue sky of southern Arizona.

Cornelius Vanderbilt. With World War II, new industries grew up. But it was the invention of low-cost air-conditioning that almost single-handedly created the boom in the "Sun Belt" of the Southwest, making it possible to live comfortbly in the desert year round. In the four decades after 1950, the population of greater Phoenix doubled — and doubled again. Many senior citizens came to the Valley of the Sun to retire. (Some communities like Sun City actually exclude residents under 55 years of age.) On the down side, Phoenix's rapid growth created the usual urban problems. The city has some of the worst air pollution in the nation, while casually controlled residential development has blighted scenic mountains and canyons.

Tourism has fueled this growth. As a sun-washed resort area, the valley now offers a whopping 50,000 swimming pools and nearly 100 golf courses, as well as a thousand tennis courts. Each year boasts more than 300 sunny days for outdoor recreation. And cultural and urban amenities aren't ignored. The **Civic Plaza** has a symphony hall and theater. The **Arizona Center** offers restaurants, nightclubs, and shops, and its three-acre terraced gardens provide a shady place to relax; this ultramodern office and entertainment complex was built in 1991 for $200 million.

Also downtown, but a world away in time, is **Heritage Square**, which boasts the city's greatest collection of turn-of-the-century houses. The 1895 **Rosson House** was the elegant home of an army doctor, built in Victorian Eastlake style with a turret and verandah. It is completely restored and open for tours. The Burgess Carriage House, next door, was designed in the architectural style of Colonial Williamsburg — quite refined for the Wild West. Other historic residences on the square are now being used as tea rooms, crafts galleries, and cafés. The granite **Arizona State Capitol** has been restored to its appearance of 1912, the year that Arizona became the nation's 48th state. Atop the building's copper dome stands a weathervane figure of Winged Victory — a statue that cowboys once regularly used for target practice with their Colt revolvers. Capitol exhibits include a wax mannequin of early Governor George Hunt seated at his desk. In 1960 the state legislature grew too big for its quarters here and moved out, and the Senate and House chambers now display historical artifacts and documents, including Arizona's statehood proclamation, items used by John Wesley Powell in exploring the Colorado River, and the Spanish-American War flag carried by the Rough Riders. More of the past is on show at the **Arizona History Room** in the First Interstate Bank building, where you'll see Arizona's first chartered bank recreated

with its original tellers' cages, furnishings, and even spittoons. The **Phoenix Museum of History** exhibits Indian crafts and items of the western frontier, including Phoenix's first printing press, an egg from a former ostrich farm, a steam locomotive, and a model of the battleship *Arizona*. The **Arizona Historical Society**'s Ellis-Shackleford House, a 1917 residence, boasts such modern conveniences as a central vacuum system, solar heating, and automatic flush toilets.

The **Arizona Mining and Mineral Museum** displays every mineral found in the state, including beautiful copper ores ranging from turquoise to malachite. The **Phoenix Art Museum** has good collections of French, Mexican, and Western art, along with the fascinating Thorne Miniature Rooms, which duplicate the interiors of historic European and American buildings. The **Pueblo Grande Museum and Cultural Park** is one of the few places where the public can see the ruins of a Hohokam village and irrigation canals, which date to the 13th century. Also in the **Phoenix area** are the Cave Creek Museum (prehistoric Indians, mining, and ranching), a zoo, and the Mystery Castle (a house built with such odd materials as automobile wheels). The city's desert botanical garden may lead you to venture again into the cactus country and mountains of the Valley of the Sun.

Three views of the historic Arizona State Capitol, topped with a statue of Winged Victory. The civic center (p. 46) and the Arizona Center (p. 47) show a blend of the old and new Phoenix.

SCOTTSDALE

CASA GRANDE RUINS N.M.

History and style come together in Scottsdale, a resort town east of Phoenix. The frontier buildings of the historic district look much like the Old West, while the trendier New West is represented by art galleries, restaurants, and boutiques with an international flair. The town is named for army chaplain Winfield Scott, who bought 600 acres near the Arizona Canal in 1888 and founded a settlement. It grew into a quiet community — no saloons or shoot-em-ups — whose residents farmed alfalfa, fruit, olives, and cotton. By the 1930s Scottsdale had attracted creative people, particularly architect Frank Lloyd Wright, who built **Taliesin West** by the McDowell Mountains; it serves as an architectural firm and school for Wright disciples, with buildings of stone, redwood, canvas, and plastic. In 1956 a former student, Paolo Soleri, established the **Cosanti Foundation**, devoted to his ideas for cities that conserve space and energy; the studios and crafts workshops are made of formed concrete.

Probably the most puzzling building in Arizona, Casa Grande is the only high-rise to survive from the prehistoric Hohokam culture. These advanced people dug irrigation canals and erected what Padre Kino, after a visit in 1694, named "the Casa Grande [Big House] — a four-story building as large as a castle and equal to the finest church in the lands of Sonora." It was built about A.D. 1350, using unreinforced caliche (a subsoil that contains calcium carbonate) and 600 wooden beams fashioned from trees that were brought from considerable distances. Today a steel roof protects the 11-room ruin from wind and sun. The Hohokam may have used this 35-foot-tall structure as an astronomical observatory to determine the summer and winter solstices. Also at the site are an unexcavated ball court, smaller structures, and a visitors center that explains what is known about this ancient culture. After using Casa Grande for only a few generations, the Hohokam mysteriously vanished in A.D. 1450.

Elegant Scottsdale, where the Old West meets the Nouveau West.

Was it an astronomical observatory? This is just one question unanswered at Casa Grande Ruins.

LAKE HAVASU

There is something wonderfully absurd about seeing 13,000 acres of water in the middle of the Arizona desert. And if the scene before your eyes includes the real London Bridge and a fake English village, it borders on the surreal. Welcome to Lake Havasu City. It began in 1964, when chainsaw manufacturer Robert McCulloch decided to build a planned community. To promote it, he bought the obsolete, 928-foot London Bridge for nearly $2.5 million; then he dismantled it, shipped the granite blocks some 10,000 miles to Lake Havusu City, and put all 10,276 stones back together again as a tourist attraction. In order for the famous bridge to span anything, the developers had to dredge a channel and create an island. Next they built an "English village," which even has a double-decker bus and a red London phone booth.

It may come as no surprise that the town planner McCulloch hired to design this fantasyland once worked for Walt Disney. At any rate, his plan worked: As an Arizona tourist draw, Lake Havasu is now second only to the Grand Canyon. Visitors come for recreation on the blue lake, including fishing (bass, crappie, catfish, bluegill), boating, and waterskiing. (On the 32-mile-long lake, it's possible to ski for an hour in one direction.) There are also plenty of spots for picnicking, and nearly 1,300 campsites. Today Lake Havasu City has more than 17,000 residents. It plays host to annual events such as a dixieland jazz festival, fishing derbies, and speedboat competitions.

Lake Havasu, the London Bridge, and the city that grew up around them have become popular tourist attractions.

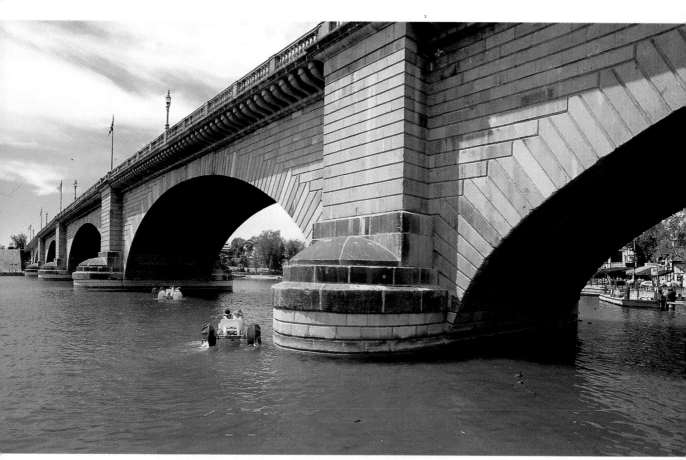

MONTEZUMA CASTLE N.M.

When explorers saw this five-story dwelling perched in a cliff above the Verde Valley in 1864, they were impressed. Believing that such a "castle" must have been built by the advanced Aztecs, they named it for Aztec ruler Montezuma. In fact, the Sinagua Indians of the 12th century built the 20-room structure. They used muscle power and ladders alone to move the materials — limestone blocks, mortar, and beams made from sycamore trees — up the cliff. Choosing a protective overhang 100 feet above Beaver Creek, they created a defensive stronghold for the 50 people who lived here. Nearby, **Castle A** had 6 stories and 45 rooms, but it has deteriorated badly. **Montezuma Well**, 10 miles northeast, is a limestone sinkhole 470 feet across, into which water flows at 1,110 gallons a minute. The Sinagua once diverted the water to irrigate their crops (and modern farmers still use it). Parts of the ancient ditches and houses can still be seen, but today the lake is home only to ducks and coots.

Built high into a cliff face, Montezuma Castle sheltered the Sinagua Indians about eight centuries ago.

SEDONA

In Sedona, great forces are at work. The powers of nature have carved a mighty fortress, with lofty walls and ancient towers of red sandstone. And New Age devotees claim that psychic and spiritual forces are focused in energy "vortexes" all around Sedona. Bell Rock is said to charge human beings with an "electric" energy, while Cathedral Rock exerts a "magnetic" energy that calms people. The 1987 celebration of the "Harmonic Convergence," an unusual planetary alignment that was supposed to usher in an age of peace and harmony, drew 5,000 people to Sedona. Some of the faithful paid $75 each to sit on Bell Rock, awaiting its departure for the Andromeda galaxy.

When visitors experience Sedona's almost magical setting of red rocks, drifting clouds, and evergreen forests, most do find themselves inspired and energized. They enjoy taking jeep tours of the high country and visiting **Oak Creek Canyon**. A few miles north of town, this canyon opens as a natural amphitheater, with Oak Creek gliding quietly through. Oaks and sycamores stand at the feet of towering red-rock walls, whose colors change with every passing hour. At **Slide Rock State Park** visitors can wear out the seats of their jeans while zipping down a natural water chute in the sandstone, then landing in a pool.

The **Chapel of the Holy Cross** — "man's church in nature's cathedral" — rises from a ridge. A follower of Frank Lloyd Wright built the chapel, whose facade is designed around a monumental cross. The town of **Sedona** offers restaurants, art galleries, and crafts shops. Many are clustered in **Tlaquepaque**, a complex that mimics a Mexican village with courtyards and fountains. Sedona has been an art center for two decades, and many resident painters and sculptors show their work here.

If the artistic backdrop behind Sedona seems familiar to you, it should: More than 80 westerns were filmed here during the 1940s and 1950s. Sedona's red-rock buttes and spires have become an indelible part of American movies.

The Chapel of the Holy Cross (below) and Cathedral Rock (following pages) capture the sense of awe that Sedona inspires.

JEROME

The ground around Jerome has yielded riches since prehistoric Indians dug here for the intense blue stone called azurite, which they used for making jewelry and pigment. Although later Indians brought Spanish explorers to see the diggings, the Europeans thought the site worthless. By 1876, however, American prospectors were staking claims on Cleopatra Hill. In 1882 New York lawyer and financier Eugene Jerome decided that the way to get money out of the ground was to pour money *into* it. He spent $200,000 to fund the United Verde Mine, which produced silver. (In return, he insisted that the town bear his name.) William Andrews Clark bought the United Verde in 1888, expanding operations with a smelter and a narrow-gauge railroad serving Jerome. When James "Rawhide Jimmy" Douglas bought the Little Daisy Mine at the base of Cleopatra Hill in 1912, he struck a five-foot-thick vein of copper. As copper prices rose during World War I, Jerome virtually minted money.

The population soared to 15,000, and Jerome lived the life of a boomtown, with gambling halls, brothels, and saloons. (A New York newspaper reporter called Jerome "the wickedest town in the West.") Jerome's layout wasn't very wise, in terms of town planning. It sat on a mountain slope, with houses placed so close together that any resident, it was said, could light a match simply by leaning out his window and striking it on his neighbor's chimney. Being built of frame lumber, the town suffered three serious fires during the late 1890s. There were floods, too, and the mines did so much underground blasting that buildings actually jumped off their foundations and fell over. The blasting, a bout of wet weather, and the instability created by more than 100 miles of mine shafts under the town finally joined to produce disaster. Jerome started to skid down the mountain. The **Sliding Jail** stopped moving about 225 feet from where it was built, having crossed a road and gone down a hillside.

Once a boomtown, with copper mines, saloons, and hotels, Jerome has nearly faded away. Today there are historic buildings and museums to explore.

Bad times came to Jerome when the Depression forced the mines to close. After brief prosperity during World War II, the last mine shut down in 1953 and the population dropped to 50. The town seemed ready to expire, but starting in the 1960s an influx of hippies, artists, retirees, and shop owners gave it another shot at life. Jerome became part historical attraction, part art colony on the wild frontier. With 400 residents, it now offers a selection of galleries, boutiques, and restaurants — including one located in a former brothel called the House of Joy.

Be sure to stroll the downtown **historic district**, full of vintage stone, brick, and wooden buildings. On Main Street try to picture the former elegance of the Barlett Hotel (now a brick shell). Or book a room at the stone Connor Hotel, which had to be rebuilt twice following the fires of the late 1890s and is still operating.

Jerome State Historic Park consists of the 1917 Douglas Mansion, built on a hilltop by flamboyant mine owner "Rawhide Jimmy" Douglas for use as both hotel and family home. Its modern innovations included steam heat and a central vacuum system, and it boasted such amenities as a wine cellar and billiard room. Upstairs you'll see a three-dimensional model of old Jerome and the honeycomb of mine shafts hidden underground. The house has a library, restored living quarters, a collection of family photos, and a reconstructed assay office; a video tells the story of Jerome's boom and bust. Outdoors stands a huge stamp mill and assorted mining equipment. The site overlooks Douglas's Little Daisy Mine, whose headframes can be seen at the foot of the hill. Nearby is the **Powder Box Church**, actually built of dynamite boxes. The Gold King Mine Museum exhibits mining machinery, from pumps to ore cars, and a replica mine shaft. The **Jerome Historical Society Museum** displays paintings, mine tools, and ore. A collection of stock certificates reveals how vast were the riches that passed through Jerome nearly a century ago.

RED CANYON

The ruins of the **Palatki** cliff dwellings offer a glimpse into the architecture of mystery. They were built more than 800 years ago by the Southern Sinagua, ancient Indians who probably blended the cultures of the prehistoric Hohokam and Anasazi people. They lived by agriculture, having learned to plant corn, squash, and beans. Like the Anasazi, they dwelled in canyons, building their homes in caves and overhangs in the rock walls.

Today you can marvel at their stone dwellings, or what remains of them, at the Palatki ruins. These remnants lie off Red Canyon, near Sedona. Here the Southern Sinagua lived around AD 1150-1250. Shortly after that time — for reasons no living person truly understands — the Sinagua vanished from the red-rock country, like grains of sand blowing in the wind. Some ethnologists believe that the Hopi Indians of modern times may be descendants of the Sinagua.

The ruins consist of two separate buildings, both of masonry construction, which are located a few hundred feet from one another. (Visitors should respect the site, which is fragile and important to contemporary Indians, by treading carefully and disturbing nothing.) In the Arizona sunset, the stones take on a pinkish glow, as they did when Palatki was a thriving community of perhaps 50 to 100 people. After the settlement was abandoned, all was quiet for centuries. No outsider made a formal survey of the Palatki ruins until archaeologist Jesse Walter Fewkes arrived in 1895. He estimated the earlier population, made measurements and drawings, and named the site Palatki, the Hopi Indians' term for "red." He gave it this name in remembrance of a Hopi myth about legendary *Palatkwabi* ("Red Land"), the place from which the Hopi believed their forefathers had come.

Does the Hopi ancestor myth actually refer to the prehistoric Southern Sinagua of Red Canyon? We may never know. But any person who admires a good mystery will enjoy the question itself, even if it is never answered.

Tread carefully at Palatki ruins, ancient home of Indians who raised corn and built stone houses on the cliffs.

LAKE MEAD

Lake Mead — the nation's largest artificial lake — resulted when **Hoover Dam** was built in 1935 to hold back the waters of the Colorado River, thus preventing floods and generating electricity. Not only is the dam beautiful in an unexpected way — with its great, icy sweep of concrete on the downstream side, and its austere simplicity amid the surrounding jumble of rock — but it also produces some amazing statistics. Hoover Dam stands 726 feet high (as tall as a 70-story skyscraper), and the 4 million cubic yards of concrete used in its construction could pave a two-lane highway from California to Florida. The dam contains as much steel as the Empire State Building. In fact, you could fill a freight train stretching all the way to Kansas City with the materials used to build Hoover Dam. Visitors can tour the dam's interior, marveling at gigantic turbines that produce four million kilowatt-hours of electricity each year.

Lake Mead itself is 110 miles long and shaped like a "Y," with one branch pointing to the Virgin River (in Nevada) and the other toward the Grand Canyon. The lake is a recreational wonderland best seen by boat, since few roads reach its shoreline. Having rented anything from a fishing boat to a houseboat, you can take a leisurely trip to enjoy the desert scenery, explore rocky gorges, and swim at sandy beaches. The lake has plenty of room for vacationers. Fishermen go after bass, trout, catfish, crappie, and bluegill. Waterskiers race across the lake. A sternwheeler makes cruises above the dam, and raft trips explore the area below, heading down Black Canyon to Willow Beach.

The north shore (on the Nevada side) has several attractions, including a **trout hatchery** (tours, exhibits) and dramatic **Virgin Basin**, whose rock formations bear colorful names such as the Haystacks and Napoleon's Tomb. The **Lost City Museum**, in Overton, Nevada, displays artifacts from prehistoric pueblo dwellings in the Moapa Valley, which was flooded under Lake Mead when the dam was built.

Hoover Dam blocks the mighty Colorado River.

Lake Mead offers watery recreation in the desert.

GRAND CANYON

"No matter how far you have wandered hitherto, or how many famous gorges and valleys you have seen, this one, the Grand Canyon of the Colorado, will seem as novel to you, as unearthly in the color and grandeur and quantity of its architecture, as if you had found it after death, on some other star..." So wrote naturalist John Muir in 1898, and his assessment still holds true. There is simply no way for the limited human brain to take in the scope and comprehend the grandeur of the canyon.

Most visitors gaze at the mighty gorge — some 277 miles long, an average 10 miles wide, and a mile down — and feel profound awe. Perhaps this feeling explains why so many of the names given to the rock formations here are sacred ones drawn from the world's religions: Holy Grail Temple, Shiva Temple, Osiris Temple, Bright Angel Point.

The Colorado River has been cutting this great gorge in the Colorado Plateau for at least five million years; meanwhile, snowmelt and rains have eroded and carved the canyon walls. Geologically, these walls are like an opened book, where it is possible to read a geological record of the earth's past 2 billion years. The story begins with granite and continues upward through schist, limestones (composed of animals from ancient seas), shales (made of silt from vanished rivers), and sandstones, including the Kaibab Sandstone (a mere 250 million years old) capping the North and South Rims.

On the clock of geologic time, man's presence here amounts to a few seconds. Archaeologists searching a cave in 1933 discovered small human figures made of willow twigs about 4,000 years ago. Two and a half millennia after that, Anasazi Indians were living in and around the canyon. No European saw the gorge until 1540, when a party from the Coronado expedition arrived. In the mid-1800s U.S. government expeditions explored the canyon, notably the 1869 and 1871 journeys of John Wesley Powell, whose party mapped the area while traveling the Colorado River in wooden boats. Although prospectors worked the canyon in the 1880s, it grew clear that more gold could be mined from tourists' pockets. A trail was hewn down to the canyon floor, and in 1901 a railroad spur was extended to the South Rim, where the rustically elegant El Tovar Hotel was built some 20 feet from the canyon's edge.

The Colorado River still carves the canyon below Toroweap Point.

Desert View stands on the canyon's South Rim.

Following pages: the view at Mather Point.

Havasu Falls refreshes the dryness of the South Rim.

An old steam locomotive rumbles into Grand Canyon Village.

Following pages:
Point Imperial, rising to 8,800 feet.

On the **South Rim** a **visitors center** introduces local geology and wildlife, which are also explained on the nearby **South Rim Nature Trail**. The **West Rim Drive** leads to Hermit's Rest, named for an 1890s miner. The **East Rim Drive** takes in spectacular Grandview Point, the Tusayan Ruin (an Anasazi pueblo of A.D. 1185), and Desert View, whose stone watchtower is decorated inside with handsome Indian designs. There are a variety of accommodations in Grand Canyon Village. To descend into the canyon itself, you can hike or board a mule for an organized ride. On the canyon floor, **Phantom Ranch** accommodates overnight guests. Outfitters offer river tours, with stops to explore side canyons, mining camps, and Indian ruins.

Because of the higher elevation of the **North Rim** (8,200 feet, compared to the South Rim's 6,876 feet), it has cool forests of spruce and pine. This side of the canyon is much quieter and less crowded, but closes to visitors during winter. A road leads to **Bright Angel Point**, where Roaring Springs emerges from a cliff far below. Many viewpoints offer panoramas, and trails enter the canyon or explore the forested area near the rim.

At the Grand Canyon you can hike from cool forests to the hot desert of the canyon floor in a single day — the equivalent of a trip from Canada to Mexico. In this range of environments many animals thrive, from mountain lions and mule deer to the tassel-eared squirrel, which lives only at the Grand Canyon. In the sky you'll see bald and golden eagles, while the canyon floor is home to jackrabbits, rattlesnakes, and collared lizards. As always, the canyon changes hues in the shifting light, silent and eternal.

WUPATKI NATIONAL MONUMENT

Among the remarkable things you'll see at this monument, which is scattered with 2,500 prehistoric sites, is the blowhole near Wupatki Ruin. Bend down and place your cheek next to this aperture in the ground, and you'll feel air rushing out (or in, depending on atmospheric conditions). This gentle wind may strike you as being the breathing of the earth itself, or perhaps the whisper of a desert god. At any rate, it seems safe to say that blowholes had some religious significance or special meaning for the people who lived here, because so many prehistoric pueblos were built near them. A network of underground fissures connects this blowhole with others in the area.

The pattern of settlement here was influenced by another natural phenomenon — the eruption of Sunset Crater, 20 miles distant. In A.D. 1064 the volcano spewed lava and blasted ash high into the sky. The resident Sinagua Indians evacuated the area, but returned a few decades later, having discovered that the wind-blown ash created a more fertile soil, ideal for farming.

The Sinagua were joined by Anasazi from northeastern Arizona, and a group of villages grew up. The inhabitants were successful at trade and farming, and the mix of cultures promoted an exchange of ideas that brought advancement to all. Although in earlier times the Sinagua had lived in brush shelters and pit houses, their new Wupatki dwellings were large, multi-storied pueblos. The largest is **Wupatki Ruin**, built around 1120, which stood three stories high and had close to 100 rooms. Archaeologist Jesse Fewkes, who mapped and photographed the ruin in 1896, gave it the Hopi

Ancient ruins at Wupatki represent what is left of villages that bustled nine centuries ago.

name *Wupatki for* "Tall House." A typical room had a fire pit in the floor and a door shaped like a "T." (To retain heat in winter, occupants hung an animal skin over the top portion, while the open lower section let in fresh air.)

A self-guided trail leads to a round depression in the ground that was presumably an open-air amphitheater, where villagers may have gathered for meetings or religious observances. A ball court nearby has been restored to its original oval shape, defined by stone walls. It resembles courts found in Aztec and Maya regions of Mexico and Central America, where players in a ritualized game tried to propel a rubber ball through a stone ring, using neither hands nor feet. The game probably had a religious function.

Three-story **Wukoki** ("Big and Wide House") **Ruin** was built of blocks of the Moenkopi sandstone on which it stands. Nine miles away rises the **Citadel**, in a commanding position on top of a narrow volcanic butte. It resembles a fortress, although its occupants don't seem to have been aggressive. Of their terraced gardens nearby, only traces remain today.

On the way to the Citadel you pass the small

Nalahiku Ruin ("House Standing Outside the Village"), which was two stories high with perhaps 14 rooms. In storage jars and burial pits, archaeologists have found the bones of owls, whose significance still remains unclear.

The fine masonry of **Lomaki Ruin** gave rise to its name, which means "Beautiful House." Scientists say the house was built around A.D. 1190, having dated the rings of trees used as roof timbers. The two-story pueblo had perhaps nine rooms and sheltered up to four families. Because the pueblo stands near a collapsed crack in the earth, it is supposed that this natural feature may have held some special meaning for the prehistoric residents.

In spring and fall, rangers lead overnight hikes — a 14-mile round trip — to **Crack-in-the-Rock Ruin**. It sits on top of a mesa with panoramic views of the Little Colorado River region, and the trail passes the ruins of other pueblos and many petroglyphs.

Doney Mountain (actually a crater) was named for a prospector who wandered the region looking for the legendary Lost Padre Mine, described by Spanish explorers in the 17th century. A trail leads to the top and a lovely view of the Painted Desert and San Francisco Peaks.

METEOR CRATER

Here is one place where you can truthfully say that a UFO ("unidentified flying object") has landed. From somewhere in space, a nickel-iron meteor weighing 60,000 tons reached our planet some 49,000 years ago. Traveling more than 40,000 miles per hour, it smashed into the ground, sending half a billion tons of shattered rock flying over the desert.

Its impact crater — the best preserved example on earth — is nearly one mile across and 600 feet deep. (The Washington Monument would fit inside.) The crater's rim rises 150 feet above the surrounding plain. Because the crater resembles those on the moon, astronauts once came here to train for moon walks.

Stop at the **visitor center** on the rim to see exhibits about the Apollo space program, as well as an assortment of meteorites; one weighing nearly 1,500 pounds was found nearby. Visitors are no longer allowed to walk the steep trail to the crater floor, but the three-mile **Rim Trail** offers good views of this remarkable hole in the ground.

SUNSET CRATER N.M.

Sunset Crater stands a thousand feet above the surrounding lava field, an odd-looking natural feature that is tinged orange and yellow by iron and sulfur. Upon seeing these colors in 1885, explorer John Wesley Powell named the cone Sunset. Created by eruption (not by a falling meteorite), it is the youngest of 400 dormant volcanoes found in the San Francisco volcanic field. When it last erupted more than 700 years ago, spewing forth an estimated billion tons of lava and ash, it forced the nearby Indians to abandon their villages around Wupatki; but the airborne ash enriched the soil so much that Indians returned to farm and settle.

The monument has a **visitor center**, where seismographs chart earth tremors worldwide; there are exhibits explaining volcanic forces. The **Lava Flow Trail** at the base of the crater explores gas vents (fumaroles), lava tubes, and even an ice cave. Hiking isn't permitted on the crater, although you may climb nearby **Lenox Crater** (7,240 feet), a cinder cone.

No meteor crater in the world is as well preserved as this one, dug about 600 feet deep.

Its last volcanic eruption was 700 years ago, but Sunset Crater still inspires respectful caution.

PETRIFIED FOREST NATIONAL PARK

A petrified forest is the sort of place that used to crop up in western tall tales. "Petrified trees?" a listener might have said. "Sure, pardner, I believe you — and I suppose they're full of petrified birds singing petrified songs!"

Yet this place is real. Or perhaps "surreal" is a better word. The national park boasts probably the biggest, most colorful assembly of petrified wood on earth. Here you'll see ancient logs that have turned to rock. How did it happen? About 225 million years ago, rivers brought fallen logs from faraway mountains and deposited them in swamps; here, dissolved minerals slowly replaced the wood cells with gleaming jasper, agate, and other semi-precious materials. Some fossilized animal remains also can be seen at the park. At the dawn of time this land was roamed by huge reptiles and amphibians, including the ferocious, meat-eating phytosaur, which resembled a crocodile.

The park's southern section holds the greatest amount of petrified wood, including such unusual examples as the **Agate Bridge**, a log span of more than a hundred feet, and the **Jasper Forest**, a broad scattering of petrified logs. You can also explore **Agate House**, a prehistoric, seven-room ruin built of blocks of colorful petrified wood; two rooms have been rebuilt. Needless to say, removing any petrified wood from the park is strictly forbidden, in order to preserve these wonders for future visitors.

In the narrow central section of the park lies the 75-room **Puerco Indian Ruin**, where prehistoric Indians lived from A.D. 1100 until 1400. These residents left mysterious petroglyphs. One shows a heron eating a frog, and apparently some images were used as solar calendars. This large and remarkable collection is located just below the mesa rim, south of the ruin. More of the enigmatic symbols can be seen on **Newspaper Rock**, a massive block of sandstone covered with what appear to be lizards, snakes, and other images.

The park's northern section takes in part of the Painted Desert.

Trees that have been transformed into rock lie scattered throughout this "forest" — one of Arizona's oddest sights.

PAINTED DESERT

The Painted Desert stretches across the northern section of Petrified Forest National Park and beyond, covering thousands of square miles. Its beauty is harsh, though painted in pastel colors. The windy plains, mesas, and hills are a canvas of light, shadow, and color, especially at dawn and dusk, when the low, warm sun washes over the landscape. The sunlight plays on layers of sediments — red, purple, blue-gray — whose tints derive from minerals such as iron and manganese. Most of the Painted Desert's natural features belong to the Chinle Formation, which was laid down early in the Triassic period some 200 million years ago.

The **Painted Desert Visitor Center**, located at the park's north entrance, shows a movie about petrified wood and the park. Heading south from here, you can drive to **Tiponi Point Overlook** and **Tawa Point Overlook**, which have great views over the Painted Desert. At Kachina Point stands the **Painted Desert Inn** (1924), whose blend of Spanish and Indian pueblo architecture is so distinctive that the inn has been preserved as a national historic landmark. Built of local southwestern materials, it contains exhibits on cultural history. Near Kachina Point, behind the inn, you can hike a trail into the **Painted Desert Wilderness**, whose 43,000 acres include colorful badlands and mesas, as well as Indian sites and petroglyphs. You can also walk to Onyx Bridge, a petrified log that is 50 feet long, or to Pilot Rock, which achieves the park's highest elevation at 6,295 feet.

At the **Pintado Point Overlook** you see an extensive lava flow, while below the **Nizhoni Point Overlook** you view soft shards of selenite gypsum, a mineral that glints in the sunshine.

Although the desert appears to be nearly lifeless, this appearance is deceiving. You may see not only prickly pear cactus but also Indian paintbrush and mariposa lilies blooming after rare rains.

Prairie dogs and jackrabbits scoot among the desert scrub, and overhead fly ravens, wrens, and larks.

The Painted Desert is a kingdom of minerals, tints, light, and shadow — a strangely haunting landscape.

CANYON DE CHELLY NATIONAL MONUMENT

Time expands at Canyon de Chelly. Sheer sandstone cliffs, shaped over many millennia, soar a thousand feet toward the sky. Gravity-defying cliff dwellings, built by the Anasazi ("Ancient Ones") around ten centuries ago, cling to the canyon walls. On the canyon floor, today's Navajo live in round dwellings called hogans, graze their sheep, and work their fields along the streambeds.

The national monument contains 26-mile-long Canyon de Chelly (pronounced "d'SHAY") and 35-mile-long Canyon del Muerto, which joins it. Both have scenic drives along their rims, with awesome views of the canyons. You can enter the gorges themselves only by foot, horse, or jeep, and only with a Navajo guide or ranger. (The one exception is the White House Ruin Trail.) This policy guards both the Anasazi ruins and the privacy of the more than 50 Navajo families who live here. The monument contains some 400 Anasazi ruins and thousands of paintings on rock walls. To get the big picture, take the **South Rim Drive of Canyon de Chelly** to the spectacular **White House Ruin**, which had 80 rooms during its occupation and is named for a plastered wall in the top section. Visitors can reach it on an easy trail. **Sliding House Overlook** has a view of a ledge where village ruins and natural water-collection basins remain. **Spider Rock Overlook** is located a dizzying 1,000 feet above the canyon floor, from which rises the pinnacle called Spider Rock, named for a Navajo deity reputed to discipline misbehaving children by eating them. On the horizon, volcanic Black Heart Butte rises 7,618 feet.

The **North Rim Drive of Canyon del Muerto** heads to **Antelope House**, a ruined village named for images of antelopes painted on the cliff nearby. At **Mummy Cave Overlook** you'll see caves named for two mummified human bodies discovered just below. **Massacre Cave Overlook** commemorates a tragic 1805 incident when Spanish soldiers killed 115 Navajos who had fled to this cliffside retreat 600 feet above the canyon floor.

Below and page 83: two views of Spider Rock; opposite: Antelope House.

Following pages: White House (p. 80-81); Tsegi Overlook surveys an area where the Anasazi ("Ancient Ones") lived a thousand years ago (p. 82).

LAKE POWELL

One of Arizona's most popular vacation spots, Lake Powell has 1,960 miles of shoreline — about 800 miles more than the California coast! Here green water meets the colorful rock formations of the desert. Towering red cliffs rise against the azure sky, and erosion has sculpted natural arches and balanced rocks. The desert extends right to the shoreline.

The gateway to the lake is Page, a town created by the boom times of construction on **Glen Canyon Dam**, completed in 1964. This dam spanning the Colorado River rises 710 feet above bedrock, is 300 feet thick at the base, and contains nearly five billion cubic feet of concrete. The **Carl Hayden Visitor Center** displays a large relief map of the area and offers tours of the dam, whose massive turbines generate more than a billion kilowatts of electrical power. The dam's major role is water storage; it contains enough to flood the state of Pennsylvania a foot deep. Lake Powell is the second-largest man-made lake in the United States.

Most of the lake lies in Utah, but Arizona has a headquarters for water recreation at **Wahweap**, a marina and tourist village. Boaters can rent a fishing skiff for a day's outing or a fully outfitted houseboat for a week's exploration of the lake. On the water you'll pass huge buttes of sandstone that rise like islands. High on the sandstone walls of side canyons you might see such delicate plants as maidenhair ferns in hanging gardens where water seeps through the porous rock. On plateaus junipers and pinyon pines grow. But on the desert level, you'll generally see only cactuses and sagebrush. Animals that live in this region, most often seen at dawn or in the evening, include western diamondback rattlesnakes, coyotes, mule deer, and mountain lions.

Just north of the Arizona-Utah border you can visit the world's largest natural rock span, **Rainbow Bridge**. Carved in salmon-pink Navajo sandstone, at 290 feet it is tall enough to fit the dome of the U.S. Capitol building beneath it.

The Colorado River is held back by Glen Canyon Dam and spanned by Glen Canyon Bridge.

Opposite: the irregular shoreline of Lake Powell. Following pages: one of the rocky formations emerging from the lake, and two views around the famous Rainbow Bridge, just north of Arizona-Utah border.

ANTELOPE CANYON

While much of Arizona fits the definition of "wide open spaces," the landscape of Antelope Canyon is quite the opposite, made up of narrow, closed spaces. Instead of the the classical terrain of the American West, with broad mesas and rocky spires silhouetted against the sunset sky, this canyon might well be the stone center of the earth. In many ways, it is a secret place, a private world.

Averaging only 30 feet deep, its rocky sides swirled like cake batter, the canyon twists for about three-quarters of a mile. The narrow crevice was sliced through a mesa by moving water and wind over an immensely long period of time. The flowing liquid carved the red Navajo sandstone into corkscrew shapes, forms that appear linked to many other spiraling designs in nature; consider the whorl of seashells, or the twisting shape of airborne seedpods.

The sun's light falls into this slot canyon in evershifting patterns, creating colors that range from pale salmon to deep burgundy, from sandy tan to the rust red of iron oxide. The lovely hues and light within Antelope Canyon account for its perennial popularity with photographers. These patient artists, both amateurs and professionals, may wait for half a day to get just the right exposure. Without a doubt, the canyon ranks among the top visual wonders of the American Southwest.

The canyon is located about three miles from the small town of Page. To make the 15-minute drive on a rough, unpaved road, motorists will need a four-wheel-drive vehicle. The gate to the site is open in summertime, and guided tours are available from Page all year round. Antelope Canyon was discovered in 1931 by a 12-year-old Navajo girl, Tsosie, who was herding sheep across the desert. Now it is privately owned by a Navajo family, who have grazing rights here. The canyon lies on the Navajo reservation, which at 25,000 square miles is the largest Indian reservation in the country, spreading clear into neighboring states Utah and New Mexico.

A twisted sculpture of a landscape, Antelope Canyon seems as if it might be on Mars, not in Arizona.

MONUMENT VALLEY

If you have seen western movies such as John Ford's 1938 *Stagecoach*, you'll realize an important truth about Monument Valley: Although these classic films feature famous actors like John Wayne, the real star is always the valley itself, a mystical place where mesas and buttes of red rock rise against an infinite blue sky. To enter this landscape is to visit another world, a place of haunting beauty. Rippling sands spread in all directions, sweeping past solitary monoliths of stone. In the warm light of sunset, the rock towers glow with what seems an internal fire.

You can read the geographical statistics, but these cannot explain the strange magnetism of Monument Valley. The valley measures 40 miles by 60 miles, and it is 5,500 feet above sea level. Once it was an inland sea, whose sandstone floor rose over time; then water and wind scoured the land, and this erosion left behind the towering buttes and jagged pinnacles of the valley today. At least one feature — Agathia Peak — is the remnant of an ancient volcano; the clue to its origin lies in its dark-colored rock, which stands out sharply against the red sandstone around it.

To see this territory, join a **guided tour** from the visitors center, which gives you a chance to see not only the famous rock formations but also a Navajo hogan, a cliff dwelling, and petroglyphs. (The Anasazi once lived in the Mystery Valley district, where many of their dwellings remain.) Motorists can also take a 17-mile self-guided scenic drive, which has many spectacular overlooks.

Begin your scenic drive near the visitors center at the **Mitten View Lookout,** gazing down over the valley's most picturesque features. West Mitten Butte is an archetypal formation, a thick tower of rock alongside a slender spire. It rises more than a thousand feet above the valley floor and is mirrored

Below: Merrick Butte in the foreground; pages 92-93: the three Buttes (West Mitten, East Mitten, Merrick) stand like mighty fortresses of stone.

Top: a view of Rain God Mesa; bottom: the sides of Camel Butte have left a block of brown rock that for its shape has been named the Thumb.

by East Mitten Butte. Merrick Butte also stands in this grouping. Look for Elephant Butte, too, and Mitchell Mesa, which is so broad that there's room for an airplane landing strip on top.

The redrock pinnacles known as the **Three Sisters** rise in stark contrast to the open sky. Standing some 1,000 feet high, they seem to be related, a family watching over the valley like statuesque goddesses. The **Totem Pole** is an isolated spire located in the area where Monument Valley comes to an end; here you'll see the last layers of the geological system composed of Hunts Mesa and Wetherill Mesa. Many other formations in Monument Valley, like Camel Butte and Spearhead Mesa, were given names that evoke their fantastic shapes. During the hours around dawn and sunset, these shapes seem to come to life as sunlight streams in at a low angle

— warm, red, and aglow. The illumination has a timeless quality, much like light playing through the stained-glass window of a cathedral. It seems to change with every passing moment.

Monument Valley makes a deeply spiritual impression on many visitors, enhanced by an awareness of the Navajo Indians' belief in the sacredness of the earth. The valley is a 29,816-acre tribal park of the Navajo, a people who have managed to preserve many of their old ways of life. You will see their hogans — round dwellings of mud and logs – and the Navajo tending sheep, weaving rugs, or selling turquoise jewelry at tables by the roadside. Many of them still cook meals over open fires and tote their babies on traditional cradleboards. The Navajo have learned to live in harmony with this harsh but haunting land.

The Three Sisters soar to a thousand feet near Mitchell Mesa.

Below and opposite page: his parched landscape is dominated by the Totem Pole and the Yei Bi Chei.

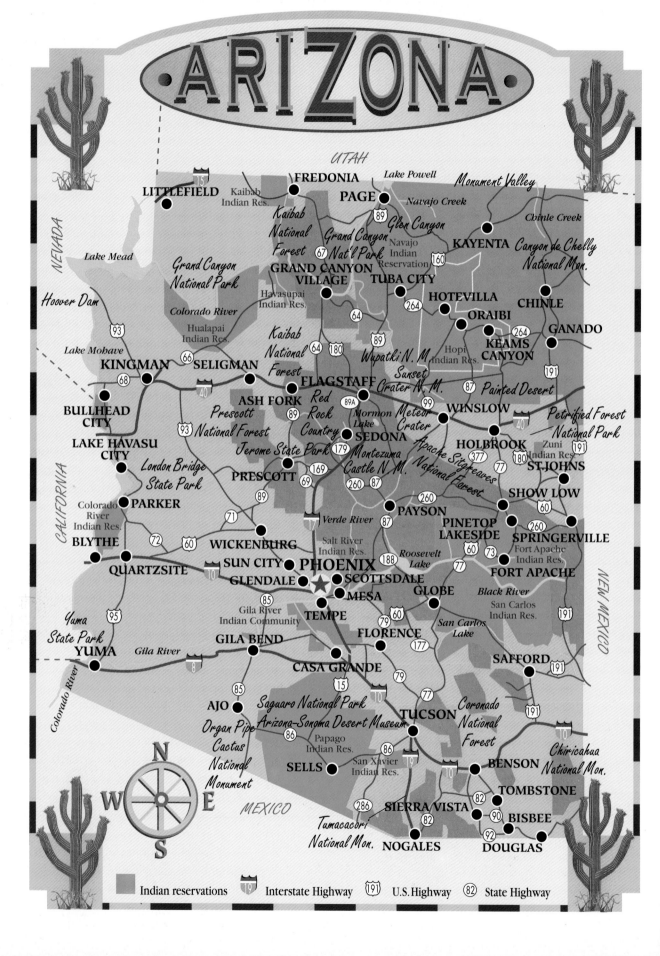

ARIZONA

UTAH

NEVADA

CALIFORNIA

NEW MEXICO

MEXICO

FREDONIA
LITTLEFIELD
Kaibab Indian Res.
Lake Powell
PAGE
Monument Valley
Navajo Creek
Chinle Creek
Kaibab National Forest
Glen Canyon
Grand Canyon Nat'l Park
Navajo Indian Reservation
KAYENTA
Canyon de Chelly National Mon.
Grand Canyon National Park
GRAND CANYON VILLAGE
TUBA CITY
HOTEVILLA
CHINLE
Lake Mead
Hoover Dam
Havasupai Indian Res.
ORAIBI
GANADO
Hualapai Indian Res.
Kaibab National Forest
Hopi Indian Res.
KEAMS CANYON
Lake Mohave
KINGMAN
SELIGMAN
Wupatki N. M.
Painted Desert
Sunset Crater N. M.
FLAGSTAFF
WINSLOW
Petrified Forest National Park
BULLHEAD CITY
ASH FORK
Red Rock Country
Meteor Crater
Prescott National Forest
Mormon Lake
HOLBROOK
Zuni Indian Res.
LAKE HAVASU CITY
Jerome State Park
SEDONA
Apache Sitgreaves National Forest
ST. JOHNS
London Bridge State Park
Montezuma Castle N. M.
SHOW LOW
PRESCOTT
Colorado River Indian Res.
PARKER
PAYSON
PINETOP LAKESIDE
SPRINGERVILLE
Verde River
Fort Apache Indian Res.
BLYTHE
WICKENBURG
Salt River Indian Res.
Roosevelt Lake
FORT APACHE
QUARTZSITE
SUN CITY
PHOENIX
SCOTTSDALE
GLOBE
Black River
San Carlos Indian Res.
GLENDALE
MESA
Yuma State Park
Gila River Indian Community
TEMPE
San Carlos Lake
YUMA
Gila River
GILA BEND
FLORENCE
SAFFORD
CASA GRANDE
AJO
Saguaro National Park
TUCSON
Coronado National Forest
Organ Pipe Cactus National Monument
Arizona-Sonoma Desert Museum
Papago Indian Res.
Chiricahua National Mon.
SELLS
San Xavier Indian Res.
BENSON
TOMBSTONE
SIERRA VISTA
BISBEE
Tumacacori National Mon.
NOGALES
DOUGLAS

Interstate Highways: 15, 40, 10, 8, 19, 17

U.S. Highways: 89, 67, 160, 264, 64, 180, 66, 68, 93, 89A, 99, 377, 191, 77, 60, 260, 71, 72, 95, 85, 86, 169, 69, 87, 188, 73, 79, 177

State Highways: 82, 90, 92, 286

Indian reservations   Interstate Highway   U.S. Highway   State Highway